Read-About® Geog

D1647714

California

By Sarah De Capua

Consultant
Nanci Vargus, Ed.D.
Primary Multiage Teacher
Decatur Township Schools, Indianapolis, Indiana

CP Children's Press®
A Division of Scholastic Inc.
New York   Toronto   London   Auckland   Sydney
Mexico City   New Delhi   Hong Kong
Danbury, Connecticut

Designer: Herman Adler Design
Photo Researcher: Caroline Anderson
The photo on the cover shows the coast of California in Monterey County.

Library of Congress Cataloging-in-Publication Data

De Capua, Sarah.
  California / by Sarah de Capua.
    p. cm. — (Rookie read-about geography)
Includes index.
Summary: Introduces the geography, animals, tourist sites, and other facts about America's westernmost state.
  ISBN 0-516-22667-3 (lib. bdg.)   0-516-27492-9 (pbk.)
  1. California—Juvenile literature. 2. California—Geography—Juvenile literature. [1. California.] I. Title. II. Series.
  F861.3 .D43 2002
  917.94—dc21

                                    2002005491

Do you know where you can find the Golden Gate Bridge?

It is in the state of California! Find California on this map. It is located in the western part of the country.

5

Many different kinds
of land can be found
in California. There are
mountains, farmland,
deserts, and forests.

There are two great mountain ranges in California. They are the Sierra Nevada and the Cascade.

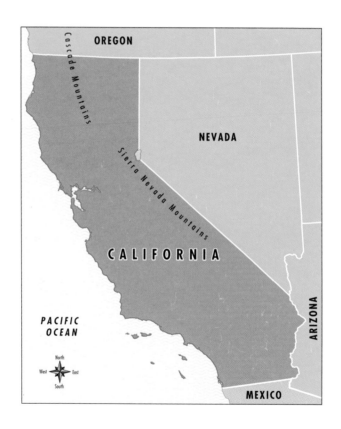

Mount Whitney is in the
Sierra Nevada mountain
range. It is the highest
point in California.

California's farmland is found east of the Sierra Nevada mountains. Fruits, vegetables, dairy products, and livestock come from this rich land.

The lowest point in the United States is called Badwater. It is located in Death Valley. Death Valley is part of the Mojave (mo-HAH-vee) Desert in southern California.

Northern California's forests are filled with giant trees called sequoia (si-KOY-ah) and redwood. They are some of the oldest and largest trees in the world.

The redwood is California's state tree.

California is next to the Pacific Ocean. Fishermen catch salmon, swordfish, shrimp, and squid in the water near California's coast.

Los Angeles

Los Angeles is California's largest city. Sacramento is the state capital.

California's other major cities include San Jose (hoh-ZAY), San Francisco (fran-SIS-ko), and San Diego.

Some people who work in California's cities have jobs in the computer industry. Others work in factories where they make aircraft, spacecraft, or cars.

Most of our country's dairy products come from farms in California. Grapes are an important crop. They are grown in vineyards. Grapes are used to make wine.

It can be cold and snowy
in northern California.

It is warm all year long
in southern California.

The California Quail
is California's state bird.
It lives in the forest.

Desert animals include
jackrabbits, lizards, and
rattlesnakes.

What is your favorite
place in California?

Words You Know

Death Valley

desert

farmland

Golden Gate Bridge

Mount Whitney

Pacific Ocean

redwood

vineyard

Index

About the Author

Sarah De Capua is an author and editor of children's books. She resides in Colorado.

Photo Credits

Photographs © 2002: David R. Frazier: 28 (Mike Penney), 6 bottom right, 6 bottom left, 11 top, 11 bottom, 12, 15, 18, 25, 30 top left, 30 top right, 31 bottom left; PhotoEdit: 17, 31 top right (Tony Freeman), 21 (Spencer Grant), 27 (Bonnie Kamin); Robert Fried Photography: 3, 6 top left, 6 top right, 14, 22, 24, 30 bottom left, 30 bottom right, 31 bottom right; Robert Holmes Photography: 9, 31 top left; Terry Donnelly: cover; Visuals Unlimited/John C. Muegge: 26.

Maps by Bob Italiano